So You Think You Know About...

TRICERATOPS?

BEN GARROD

So You Think You Know About...

TRICERATOPS?

Kane Miller
A DIVISION OF EDC PUBLISHING

First American Edition 2019
Kane Miller, A Division of EDC Publishing

First published in the UK in 2018 by Zephyr, an imprint of Head of Zeus, Ltd

Text © Ben Garrod, 2018
Paleo Art © Scott Hartman, 2018, and Gabriel Ugueto, 2018
Cartoon illustrations © Ethan Kocak, 2018
Designed by Sue Michniewicz

The moral right of Ben Garrod to be identified as the author and of
Scott Hartman, Gabriel Ugueto and Ethan Kocak to be identified as
the artists of this work have been asserted.

For information contact:
Kane Miller, A Division of EDC Publishing
PO Box 470663
Tulsa, OK 74147-0663
www.kanemiller.com
www.usbornebooksandmore.com
www.edcpub.com

Library of Congress Control Number: 2018958197

Printed and bound in the United States of America
1 2 3 4 5 6 7 8 9 10
ISBN: 978-1-61067-860-5

For my mum and dad,
always helping me believe in myself

CONTENTS

Dr. "Boneboy" Ben is a very special geek indeed. Not a week goes by when I don't get on the phone to ask Dr. Ben a question about obscure, strange aspects of biology, and he always has the answers. The reader of this book is very lucky to have such a terrific teacher!

The study of science makes sense of everything in our world. Science makes everything work, and the genius scientists behind technology genuinely are the most powerful people in the world . . .

INTRODUCTION
by Steve Backshall

Paleontology, or dino science, is not just about unearthing old stone bones, it's about understanding our planet, and everything that has ever lived on it. By bringing it to life for a new generation, Dr. Ben is connecting you to our past, and making you a part of the knowledge of our future. As he says, there is nothing wrong with being clever; you should embrace your inner geek, and see the world as a puzzle waiting to be solved . . .

Enjoy the adventure.

Hey, Guys

"What do you want to do when you grow up?"

I used to hate that question and I still do. It's great to have an idea, but if you don't, adults can sometimes make you feel that you need to decide. When I was little, I wanted to be a marine biologist, then I wanted to be a paleontologist (a scientist who studies fossil animals and plants and extinct species) and then, when I was ten, I wanted to be a doctor specializing in gross diseases . . . weird, right? Not as weird as my little brother – he wanted to be a police car . . . not even a police officer but an actual police car! Well, he didn't become a vehicle and I didn't become a pathologist. I was 17 years old when I changed my mind again and had a panic about what I was going to do "when I grew up."

"**What do you love?**" my mum asked. I told her that I loved medicine, but she said, "No, you love the thought of working in medicine." She asked me again what I really loved. My answer was simple: "**I love nature**."

"Then do that. **Do something you love**. Try to have a job that means each day you smile and look forward to it."

I never forgot that. My mum said that it didn't matter if I didn't have a plan about what to do after school. She said that I should see life like a **journey** with lots of pathways. "You have no idea where these paths will take you, but go and **explore** them, try different things." And that's what I've done ever since. I've had more jobs than I can remember – I've been an undertaker, a waiter, I've researched **sharks**, followed **polar bears**, saved **chimpanzees** and **orangutans**, presented TV documentaries on **skeletons**, **dinosaurs** and **robots** and worked in a zoo. Now, I teach at a university and I'm writing these books about dinosaurs for you. I've worked in South America, the Caribbean, the Arctic, across Africa and in Asia. I

don't know what I will be doing next year or even next week and still have no idea what I will do when I "grow up" (and I am a grown-up, I think).

If it's possible, I want you to be the same – try as many things as you can to find out what you love. Maybe you want to save rare eagles (so start bird-watching now), or you want to design robots (begin looking at how circuits work) or you want to be a paleontologist (get a notebook and go looking for fossils). That's what science is about – you don't always have all the answers (and that's OK) and you often end up doing something totally different than what you planned. And that's OK too. Science is fun because it's a weird and wonderful journey and you never know what you will discover.

I wanted to write *So You Think You Know About . . . Dinosaurs?* in a way that is **exciting** and full of the **newest science**. Each book is about a single species: its anatomy, habitats and behavior. We look at where and when they lived, which species they were related to and how each species evolved unique and interesting adaptations. The thing about paleontology is that we still have so much to learn and what we do know is **constantly changing**. That's part of the fun – it's like a jigsaw puzzle. Every day scientists are developing new techniques and **discovering new fossils** and this makes sure that paleontology is one of the most exciting areas in science. I hope you enjoy reading about *Triceratops*, one of the coolest of all the dinosaurs.

Let's get geeky!

Ben

CHAPTER 1

Dinosaur Definitions

WHAT *IS* A DINOSAUR?

To build a full picture of dinosaurs, it helps to know not only what a dinosaur is but also how all the dinosaurs were related to each other. We have had a good look at what a dinosaur actually is and isn't in *Tyrannosaurus rex*, but here, I want to jump ahead a bit and look into the dinosaur "family."

In science, we love to divide big groups into smaller groups. This helps us understand how the big groups work and how the smaller groups are related. Take spoons, for example. They belong to a big group called cutlery. This group includes knives and forks as well. Looking at just the spoons, we can split them into two more groups: little spoons and big spoons. Let's focus on big spoons, like a soup spoon, or a dessert spoon. There can be lots of options within the big group, but we can choose one to focus on. It's important to understand how things, like species, are classified. In science, this is called **taxonomy**.

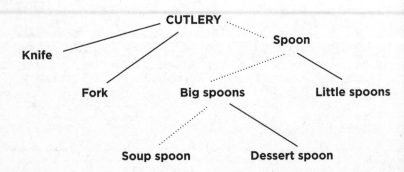

It might not come as a big surprise that understanding how we classify dinosaurs is trickier than how we separate spoons. Although scientists know of about 1,000 species of dinosaurs so far (not including the 10,000 or so species of birds around today), knowing who's who has been difficult. It's always been pretty much agreed that there is a single big split in dinosaur classification. This is between the "bird-hipped" Ornithischia dinosaurs (*or-nee THIS-kee-aah*) and the "lizard-hipped" Saurischia (*sore-RISS kee-aah*).

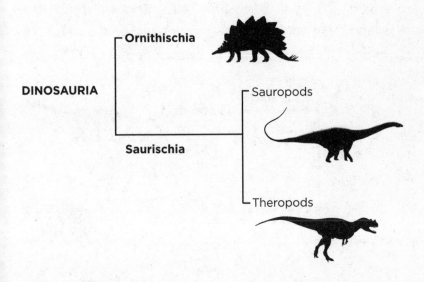

The Ornithischia are the horned dinosaurs like *Triceratops* and armored dinosaurs like *Stegosaurus* and *Ankylosaurus*. The Saurischia are split into a further two groups. First, there are the sauropods (everything from *Diplodocus*

and *Brachiosaurus* to *Argentinosaurus*). Then there are the theropods (like *Tyrannosaurus rex*, *Spinosaurus*, *Velociraptor* and *Troodon*). If you look at the family tree on page 17, you can see that the sauropods and theropods are more closely related to each other than they are to the Ornithischians.

Then, science at its best happened. A young scientist was investigating a topic in paleontology and questioned even the very basics of what we thought we knew. He wondered, "What if we've been thinking about dinosaurs all wrong?" He and his colleagues looked at lots of fossils again and this time, the family tree looked very different.

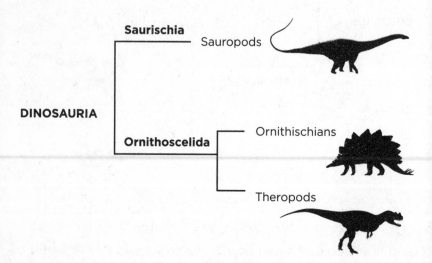

Suddenly, the sauropods and theropods were split apart. The sauropods were out on their own in the "saurischia"

(a group of one type). In this new family tree, the theropods and the ornithischians are paired up in a new group called the Ornithoscelida (*orn-nitho-skelidda*). This new idea changed everything we thought we knew about dinosaurs, but we're not entirely sure if this new research is 100 percent accurate just yet. It's not that there's anything wrong with it, but for big things like this in science, it sometimes takes a while for us to be certain.

Hey, wait . . . while I was writing this chapter there has been more news that might mean we'll be reclassifying dinosaurs in yet another different way. I'll keep you posted on what happens.

We still use the first version of the main dinosaur groups, but it's very exciting to think that might change soon. The dinosaurs are a fascinating group, but if we still aren't sure about this sort of stuff, imagine how much more there is to learn.

DEFINITELY DINOSAURS

It may seem odd but we don't have a single definition of what a dinosaur is. This is because there were so many different types. Some were small, some were huge. Some had two legs, some had four. Some were hunters and others were herbivores. With so many differences, it makes it hard to have a set of rules that works for every fossil. Instead, we use rough guidelines – if a fossil has most of the following, then scientists can be pretty certain they're dealing with a dinosaur.

1. Dinosaurs have two holes behind each eye toward the back of the skull. This means they are diapsids. If you're wondering, we (as mammals) belong to the synapsid group, all of which have only one hole behind each eye. When you're in your local museum, look at any dinosaur skeleton. The skull should have two holes just behind the eye.

2. Dinosaurs all had straight legs. Next time you see a crocodile when you're out for a walk, have a look at its legs (just don't get too close). Rather than legs that stand straight like ours, their legs bend out in the middle somewhere. All reptiles with legs, such as

CROCODILE   DINOSAUR

crocs and their relatives and many lizards, have legs that look the same – they come out from the body to the side and then go down.

20

All dinosaurs (whether with four legs or two) walked with their legs held in a straight line beneath their body. This meant dinosaurs could breathe easily as they walked or ran – great for chasing other dinosaurs, or running away from them. It also allowed them to become much bigger than if they had legs with a bend in the middle.

3. Dinosaurs had short arms. We all know that *Tyrannosaurus rex* and its relatives had teeny arms, but almost every dinosaur had forelimbs slightly shorter than you might expect. Have a look at your arms – the upper arm bone (humerus) is only a little longer than the two lower arm bones (radius and ulna). In dinosaurs, the radius is nearly always at least 20 percent shorter than the humerus.

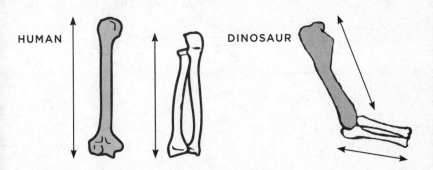

HUMAN   DINOSAUR

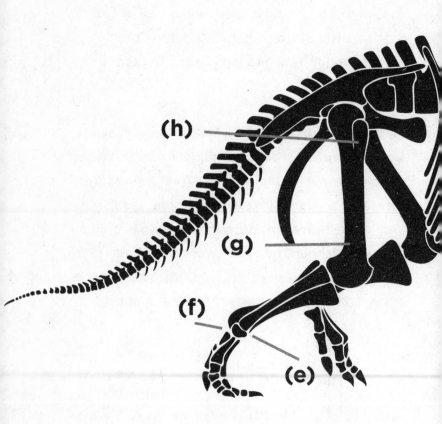

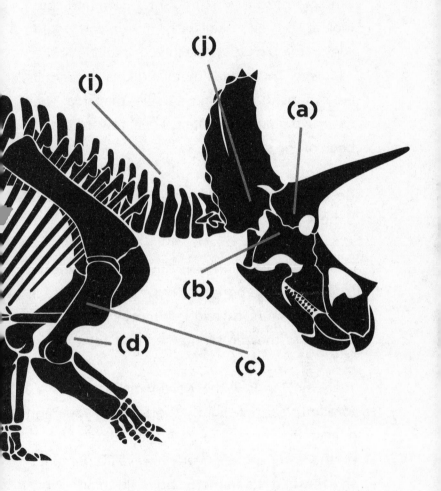

(j)

(i)

(a)

(b)

(d)

(c)

DINO CHECKLIST

 Dino diapsids. If you had X-ray vision and could look at your own skull in the mirror, you would see that you have a hole in your skull behind each eye. This means that we (like all mammals) are **synapsids**. But dinosaurs are **diapsids**. They have two holes behind each eye, toward the back of the skull. **(a)**

 Between the two holes behind the eye, there is a dimple (called a **fossa**) in the bone. **(b)**

 There is a ridge along the edge of the **humerus** (the upper arm bone) for big muscles to attach to. In dinosaurs, this ridge is more than 30 percent of the way along the bone. **(c)**

 Teeny tiny arms. Almost every dinosaur had **forelimbs** (arms) slightly shorter than you might expect. For most dinosaurs, the **radius** bone (in the lower arm) is nearly always 20 percent shorter than the **humerus** bone (in the upper arm). **(d)**

 The ridge on the **tibia** (shin bone) curves to the front and outward. **(e)**

At the place where the **fibula** (one of the lower leg bones) joins the ankle, there's a little dip on the ankle bone. **(f)**

Straight legs. Have a look at people around you – their legs come straight down from their body, not out to the side like a crab. Dinosaurs were the same – their legs were straight, not out to the side. All reptiles (well, those with legs) have legs out to the side. **(g)**

The ridge (called the **fourth trochanter**) on the **femur** (thigh bone), which the big leg muscles attach to, is big and looks sharp. **(h)**

Most of the neck bones (**vertebrae**) have extra bits of bone that look like a diagonally backward-facing wing on each side. These bits of bones are called "**epipophyses**" (*eppi-pofe ee-sees*). **(i)**

The bones at the back of the skull do not meet in the middle. **(j)**

Some of these things are obvious on some fossils and almost impossible to see on others. To spot them, you have to *really* know what to look for. Have a good look at a dinosaur fossil next time you're at your local museum and then look at a crocodile or alligator skeleton and maybe a bird. Can you check these things off in all these skeletons?

The *Triceratops* skeleton has what's needed for you to identify a dinosaur. Remember,  not every single dinosaur has all the clues, but they will have most of them. See how many you can check off. How easy are they to spot?

CHAPTER 2

Dinosaur Detectives

Triceratops

If dinosaur "celebrities" existed, then *Triceratops* was among the most famous, along with *Tyrannosaurus* and *Diplodocus*. The *Triceratops* is one of the most recognizable of any dinosaur.

It was a four-legged herbivore, larger than a rhinoceros but smaller than an elephant. It had one horn above its nose, two long horns above the eyes and a large round crest made from bone that stretched around the back of the skull. The name *Triceratops* comes from three Greek words. "Tri" means *three*, "kéras" means *horn* and "ops" means *face* – so *Triceratops* means *"three-horned face."* It is the best known of all the horned dinosaurs, called the "ceratopsid" dinosaurs.

It lived in an area that is now North America about 68 million years ago, in the Maastrichtian (*Maz trick-she-an*) stage of the Late Cretaceous. This was the very last stage in the Cretaceous, before the asteroid struck and wiped out all the dinosaurs (not including the birds). This means that *Triceratops* was one of the very last non-avian (non-bird) dinosaurs alive on Earth.

The first *Triceratops* fossil was found in Colorado in 1887. It was sent to the famous fossil hunter Charles Marsh. No one had ever seen a *Triceratops* before and Marsh thought that the fossil was the huge horns from a type of bison, a wild relative of the cow. A year later, he realized that there were such things as horned dinosaurs. It was only after a third skull was found (which was much more complete than the first two) that Marsh said he had fossils from this new dinosaur, the "Ceratops."

Imagine there being so many fossils from a single species in one area. Between 2000 and 2010, nearly 50 complete (or almost complete) *Triceratops* skulls were discovered in that same part of the US. One paleontologist said, "It is hard to walk out into the Hell Creek Formation and not stumble upon a *Triceratops* weathering out of a hillside." Nowadays, we know that the *Triceratops* is a distinct type of dinosaur, but did you know that there are two different types of *Triceratops*? There are two species – *Triceratops horridus* and *Triceratops prorsus*.

One of the most obvious things about the horned dinosaurs, including *Triceratops*, are their horns and frills. There is a lot of variation between species, which helps scientists separate them. We still don't know exactly what the horns and frills were for. We have some ideas – maybe they were used to fight off predators, or to help the dinosaurs warm up or cool down. Maybe they were used in displays to other horned dinosaurs.

FAMILY TREE

The technical term for the horned dinosaurs is the Ceratopsidae, so *Triceratops* was a ceratopsid dinosaur. There were lots of them, of different shapes and sizes. All the horned dinosaurs were four-legged herbivores from the Cretaceous period. Most were found in what is now North America but one or two have been discovered in Asia.

So, what did these dinosaurs have in common? Well, they had horns and long triangular frills around the edge of their skulls. They had some specialized eating equipment – rows of teeth at the back of their mouths that sheared like scissors and a big hooked beak at the front of their mouth.

PACHYRHINOSAURUS

ALBERTACERATOPS

STYRACOSAURUS

ANCHICERATOPS

TRICERATOPS

PENTACERATOPS

CHASMOSAURUS

TOROSAURUS

CENTROSAURUS

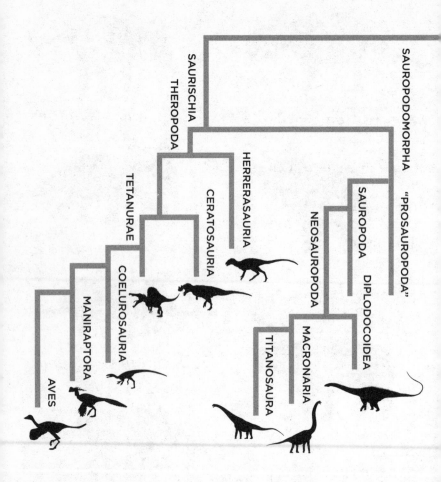

More horned dinosaurs are being discovered all the time and currently we know of more than 65 species. It's a group that evolved quickly with lots of different-looking species.

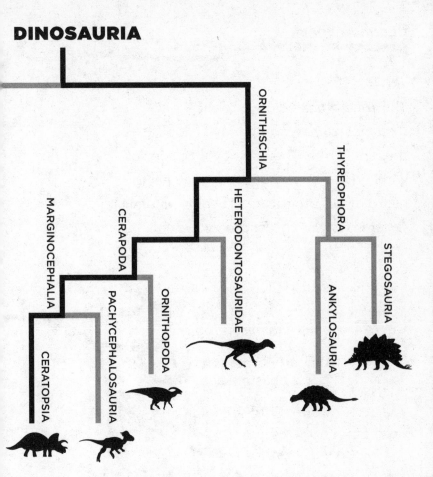

DINOSAURIA

ORNITHISCHIA

THYREOPHORA

MARGINOCEPHALIA

CERAPODA

HETERODONTOSAURIDAE

STEGOSAURIA

PACHYCEPHALOSAURIA

ORNITHOPODA

ANKYLOSAURIA

CERATOPSIA

There are two big groups within the horned dinosaurs. The Centrosaurinae had good-sized horns around their noses and their skull frills were more rectangular. Often, the spines on the back of the frill looked more developed and complex. The other group, the Ceratopsinae (or Chasmosaurinae) had long, triangular frills and big horns above their eyes.

33

Chasmosaurinae

The *Triceratops* belongs to the
Chasmosaurinae group. Have a look at
the family tree. There are a lot of species
within the group – some you may have
heard of but others are probably unfamiliar.
Triceratops was the last to evolve.

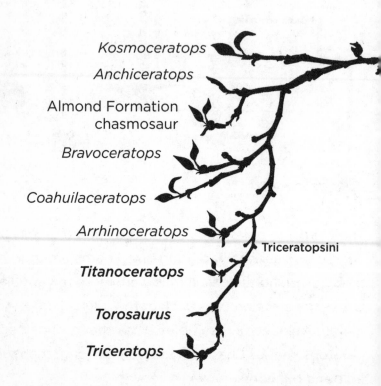

Kosmoceratops

Anchiceratops

Almond Formation
chasmosaur

Bravoceratops

Coahuilaceratops

Arrhinoceratops

Triceratopsini

Titanoceratops

Torosaurus

Triceratops

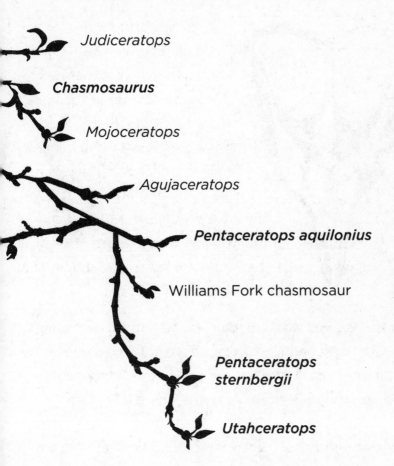

Mercuriceratops

Judiceratops

Chasmosaurus

Mojoceratops

Agujaceratops

Pentaceratops aquilonius

Williams Fork chasmosaur

Pentaceratops sternbergii

Utahceratops

You can see they were closely related to *Torosaurus* and *Titanoceratops*. These made up the Triceratopsini dinosaurs, within the bigger family of the horned (ceratopsid) dinosaurs.

TRICERATOPS **RELATIVES**

Chasmosaurus (*Kaz-mo saw-rus*) "hollow lizard"

This ceratopsid dinosaur had a skull roughly 42.6 ft. long and a frilled crest that was longer and wider at the back than the front. The big holes in the crest gave it the name "hollow" or "opening" lizard. Unlike many horned dinosaurs, the crest on *Chasmosaurus* was roughly in line with its nose or beak. The back of the crest was V-shaped and the sides were pretty straight.

Chasmosaurus was a medium-sized horned dinosaur, 14–16 ft. long and 1.7–2.2 tons in weight (the same as a big family car). It was alive in the Late Cretaceous and was found in North America. There were two species of *Chasmosaurus* – *Chasmosaurus russelli* and *Chasmosaurus belli*. Both were found in what's known as the Dinosaur Provincial Park of Alberta, in Canada. Within this area, *Chasmosaurus russelli* fossils are found in layers below *Chasmosaurus belli* fossils, which shows that *Chasmosaurus russelli* was around first.

Titanoceratops (*Ti-tanno serra-tops*)
"titanic horn face"

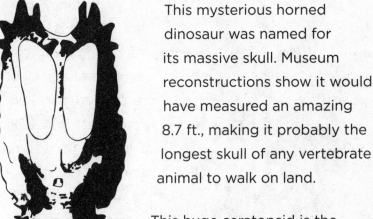

This mysterious horned dinosaur was named for its massive skull. Museum reconstructions show it would have measured an amazing 8.7 ft., making it probably the longest skull of any vertebrate animal to walk on land.

This huge ceratopsid is the first known member of the Triceratopsini, the smaller group within the ceratopsid family tree that would eventually lead to the *Triceratops*. It lived between 74.7–73.5 million years ago during the Late Cretaceous and was found in what is now New Mexico.

Everything we know about *Titanoceratops* comes from one fossil discovery, with parts of the skeleton, lower jaw and the fairly complete skull. Scientists estimate it would have been around 22 ft. in length and weighed over 7 tons.

Styracosaurus (*Sty-racco saw-rus*) "spear-tip lizard"

This very fancy-looking horned dinosaur had 4–6 long horns coming up from the back of its crest. It also had a small horn on each cheek and a 23-in. horn on the end of its snout. The horns look quite different on each of the *Styracosaurus* fossils found. Some researchers think the nose horn was about 23 in. long, but others think it was half this length.

Styracosaurus lived about 75.5–75 million years ago, during the Late Cretaceous. Fossils have been found in Alberta in Canada and Montana in the United States. Although not a huge ceratopsid, *Styracosaurus* was big, reaching lengths of 18 ft. and weighing 3–5 tons. That's bigger than a white rhino but smaller than an African elephant. Scientists think the horns were used for extreme displays between these animals, which probably lived in large herds. Very possibly, adult males would have used them to display to other males, so that they could become dominant and mate with females.

Wendiceratops (*Wen-dee serra-tops*)
"Wendy horn-face"

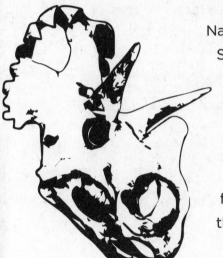

Named after Wendy Sloboda who found the first fossils of this species. Unlike many of the horned dinosaurs, this species had a series of hooked horns, curving forward from the top of the crest.

This medium-sized ceratopsid lived 79–78.7 million years ago and fossils have been found in Alberta, Canada. It is the earliest known species of horned dinosaur to have a tall nose horn. *Wendiceratops* would have weighed about 1.1 tons and been almost 20 ft. long. This species has been described from several adult and juvenile fossils found from one site.

So You Think You Know About Dinosaurs?

How many species of birds are there
around today?

•

Was a *Triceratops* larger or smaller
than an elephant?

•

How many species of horned dinosaurs
do we currently know about?

•

How many horns did a *Triceratops* have and where?

•

Where have most *Triceratops* fossils
been found?

*All the answers are in the text
and at the back of the book.*

CHAPTER 3

Dinosaur
Discoveries

WHEN AND WHERE

WHEN AND WHERE

The times when dinosaurs existed can be split into three main chunks or "periods" of time. These are the **Triassic period**, the **Jurassic period** and the **Cretaceous period**. *Triceratops* was around toward the end of the Cretaceous, just before the famous asteroid strike. They actually appeared about 68 million years ago, during what we call the Maastrichtian (*Maz trick-she-an*) stage of the Late Cretaceous.

In 2009, scientists helped show that the two species, *Triceratops prorsus* and *Triceratops horridus*, did not live together at the same time. Fossils from the two species are found in different levels in the Hell Creek Formation, the main area for *Triceratops* fossils. Because these different layers were laid down at different times in history, we know that the two species never met.

Triceratops fossils have been found in Colorado, Montana, South Dakota and Wyoming, and in the Canadian provinces of Saskatchewan and Alberta.

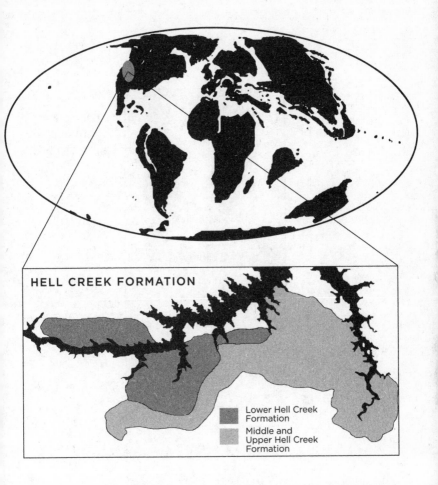

HELL CREEK FORMATION

Lower Hell Creek Formation

Middle and Upper Hell Creek Formation

Many of the *Triceratops* fossils known have been found in the Hell Creek Formation. This is an area that was a system of freshwater and brackish habitats. There would have been bogs, marshes, meadows and plains. Lots of fossils from different types of animals (dinosaurs, pterosaurs, fish, amphibians, snakes, lizards, turtles,

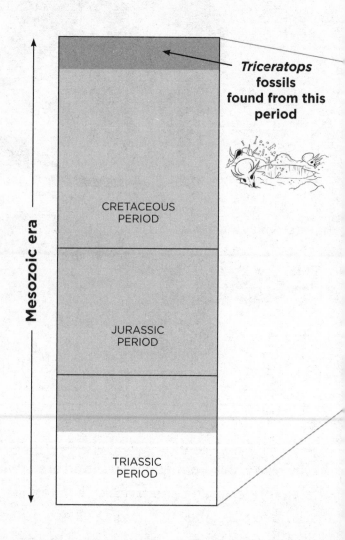

Triceratops
**fossils
found from this
period**

Mesozoic era

CRETACEOUS
PERIOD

JURASSIC
PERIOD

TRIASSIC
PERIOD

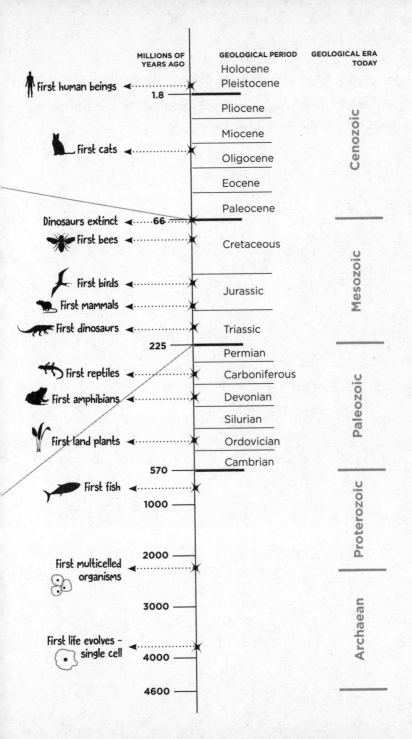

crocodiles, insects and mammals) have been found there and it is one of the most studied places in the world for fossils and extinct species.

What was the environment like when dinosaurs were around?

So many people work with dinosaurs –
from amateur collectors to world-famous scientists.
Some go looking for fossils in the ground, others study
them in laboratories and some recreate them
as incredible pieces of artwork.

DR. SHAENA MONTANARI

Paleoecologist

Science Policy Fellow,
National Science Foundation (US)

Shaena works in science communication, education,
and outreach. She trained as a paleontologist and is
interested in exploring what fossil teeth and bones
can tell us about prehistoric environments.

We know so much about dinosaurs from their fossils –
were their teeth sharp or blunt? Did they walk on two
legs or four? Were they small or huge? I'm interested in
discovering more about how they lived. What exactly
did they eat and what kinds of environments did they
live in millions of years ago? A more accurate way to say
this is that I look at their ecology.

I've always been interested in what
kind of habitats extinct animals like
dinosaurs lived in – dry and cold?
Hot and humid? Luckily, there are
a few ways we can use
fossils and other clues
to figure this out.

In my research, I often use parts of extinct animals,
like their teeth, bones and eggshells, and look at the
different chemicals within them. The amount of certain
elements in teeth, like carbon and oxygen, can show
us what kind of plants the animal was eating and how
much water it was drinking. This can then tell us what
type of habitat the animals lived in.

I mainly looked at pieces of dinosaur eggshells and
teeth from Mongolia. Many types of dinosaur lived in

 Mongolia about 80 million years ago, from meat-eating theropods like *Velociraptor* to vegetarians like *Protoceratops*.

Measuring the amount of carbon and oxygen in eggshells from *Velociraptor* and teeth of *Protoceratops* allowed me to discover that these dinosaurs were thriving in a hot, dry environment 80 million years ago – quite similar to what Mongolia is like today!

Paleontologists can also look at clues in rocks and sediments. Different types of microscopic pollen grains can tell us what types of plants were most common in the area. If we study pollens like this and look at the different chemicals in eggshells and fossil bones, we can also figure out how climates and environments changed, and how this might have affected the dinosaurs.

Dinosaur fossils are not just interesting because they belong to cool-looking, long-extinct creatures, but also because there is a huge amount of hidden information locked inside their bones that scientists today can extract to learn more about where they lived and what they ate!

CHAPTER 4

Delve into a Dinosaur

ANATOMY OF *TRICERATOPS*

THE BONES

You don't need to be an expert to recognize a *Triceratops* – it's one of the easiest dinosaurs to identify simply because of its skull.

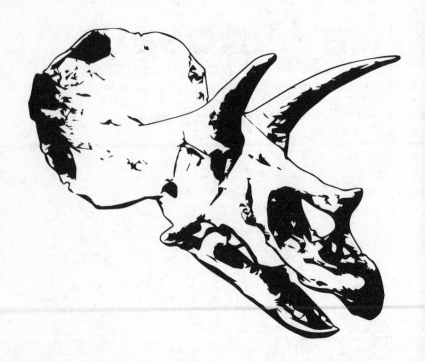

THE SKULL

Triceratops was one of the largest land animals. As well as having the distinctive horns and frill, its skull was special because it was so big – it could be one-third of the entire length of the body. The largest *Triceratops* skull found measured just over 8 ft. in length. Usually, adult skulls were about 6.5 ft. in length. The two species of *Triceratops*, *T. horridus* and *T. prorsus*, were closely related and although they looked similar, their beaks and snouts were different. *Triceratops prorsus* had a longer snout and the horn above the nose was also longer. Although not always the case, the longer horns above the eyes often look straighter on skulls.

Triceratops horridus

Triceratops prorsus

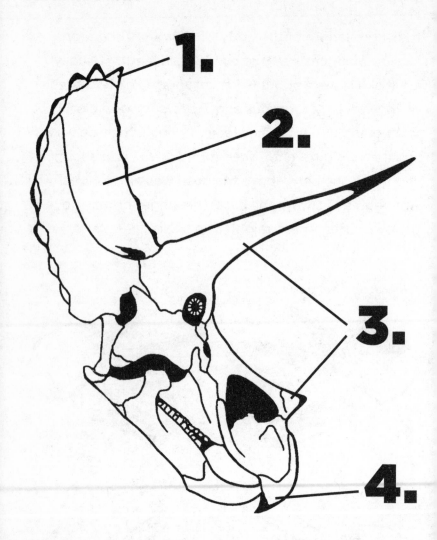

1. Some horned dinosaurs had a massive **bony crest** or **frill** at the back of the skull, but the *Triceratops* crest was quite a short one. It had a row of special bones that looked like little spikes running along the edge of the frill, making it look like a crown. These bones are only found in horned dinosaurs and are called **epoccipitals** (*ee-pock sip-ittals*). They were probably **used for display** and may have **helped different species tell each other apart**.

2. Many of the ceratopsids had **frills with holes**. These holes are called **fenestrae** (*fen-ess tray*) from the Latin word for windows. Although we are not certain, they were probably covered with muscle and tendons and you wouldn't have been able to see through them despite their name. **Species with larger frills would have had much stronger jaw muscles**, so although they would have had a powerful bite, it wouldn't have been as big as something like a *Titanoceratops*. A *Triceratops* had a smaller frill than a *Titanoceratops* and would have had a weaker bite.

3. The skull had **one horn above the nose** and **two very long horns above the eyes**. The long horns grew up to about 40 in. One very big skull had horns 45 in. long.

4. *Triceratops* had a mouth ending in a beak, which looked like a parrot's beak. This part of the mouth had no teeth and was probably an adaptation that allowed the animal to grasp and pluck at leaves and branches.

The rest of the mouth did have teeth and these were incredibly specialized. *Triceratops* were herbivores and their teeth were perfect for eating tough vegetation. All the teeth had two roots and were arranged in groups called dental batteries.

These dental batteries were unique to the ceratopsid dinosaurs. Single teeth were locked together, arranged in horizontal rows and vertical columns, a bit like a cuboid made up from smaller cubes.

There were usually three to five teeth in each column. Only one of these columns was used at any time. The other two were replacement columns. The teeth of a *Triceratops* were continuously replaced throughout its lifetime. As they were worn smooth by rough vegetation, they would have fallen out and been replaced by new, sharper teeth.

An adult *Triceratops* could have up to 40 columns of teeth in each side of its jaw and in the top and bottom jaw. That's 430–800 teeth but only a small number were actually used at any time.

Unlike most dinosaurs, *Triceratops* skull fossils are much more common than fossils from the rest of the body. We think this is because the *Triceratops* skull was so solidly put together, while the skull of something like a *Diplodocus* had a more delicate structure.

The teeth that were in use were very sharp because they slid past each other and sharpened themselves, like scissors, easily slicing through the toughest leaves and plant stems.

THE SKELETON

The two species of *Triceratops* were large quadrupedal (four-legged) dinosaurs, about the size of a very big elephant (but a bit longer). They had interesting skeleton adaptations that helped them become some of the most successful herbivorous dinosaurs.

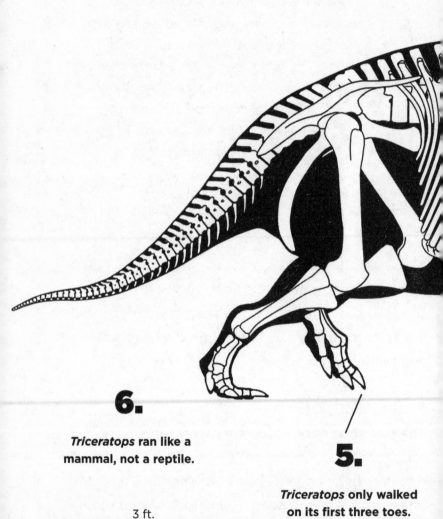

6.

Triceratops ran like a
mammal, not a reptile.

5.

Triceratops only walked
on its first three toes.

3 ft.

1.

Triceratops had a sturdy build and low center of gravity. It had two horns above its eyes and one above its nose.

2.

Elbows would have been slightly angled outward and bent.

3.

Powerful, thick limb bones and very short feet.

4.

The feet didn't face forward but instead faced outward, away from the body.

1. *Triceratops* had a sturdy build and low center of gravity.

Many people assume horned dinosaurs used their crests and horns to defend themselves from predators, but when scientists looked at the evidence, it wasn't quite right. Many species had crests that were either weak or had holes in them, and their horns were close to their face, meaning that if they were for defending themselves from predators, it would have probably been too late by the time a hungry theropod was almost on top of them.

2. Elbows would have been slightly angled outward and bent.

Even though it's pretty obvious that *Triceratops* was a quadruped, for a long time there was disagreement about exactly how it walked. It was originally thought that the front legs came out at an angle from the body (like a lizard's legs) and that they sprawled to support the very heavy head. Nowadays, better reconstructions of the skeletons show they were more upright. The elbows would have been slightly angled outward and bent, similar to the skeleton of a rhinoceros.

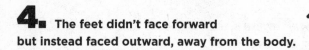

3. Powerful, thick limb bones and very short feet.

Their front feet had three claws and their hind feet had four claws.

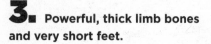

4. The feet didn't face forward but instead faced outward, away from the body.

Some quadrupedal dinosaurs (like the sauropods) had complicated-looking front and hind feet, but *Triceratops* (and other horned dinosaurs) had feet that looked simple, even basic. Their feet didn't face forward as in many dinosaur species but instead faced outwards, away from the body. This "toes-out" style is thought of as a primitive feature.

5. *Triceratops* only walked on its first three toes.

Even though there were five toes on each front foot, *Triceratops* only walked on the first three toes. The other two were higher up the foot and did not have claws. The number of bones at the end of each toe (called the phalanges) differed as well. If you start at the toe on the side closest to the chest, it had two bones. The next had three, the next had four, then three again and finally, the little toe, on the outside of the body, had only one bone.

6. *Triceratops* ran like a mammal, not a reptile.

The skeleton has helped scientists to estimate how fast *Triceratops* could run. They used the positions of the bones as well as fossilized footprints to predict that it ran like a mammal and not like a reptile. Because the limbs look like those of a rhinoceros, some scientists think *Triceratops* may have been able to run as fast as a rhino – up to 34 mph. If you're not sure how fast that is, the fastest human can run at 28 mph.

Rhinoceros skeleton

Triceratops **skeleton**

THE BODY

1.

We still don't know
what the horns and
frills were used for.

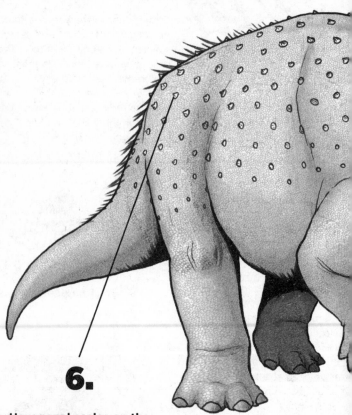

6.

Hexagonal scales on the
rest of the body may have
held a quill.

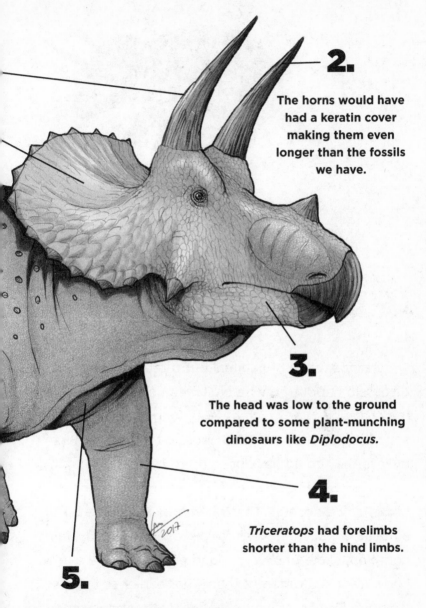

2.

The horns would have had a keratin cover making them even longer than the fossils we have.

3.

The head was low to the ground compared to some plant-munching dinosaurs like *Diplodocus.*

4.

Triceratops had forelimbs shorter than the hind limbs.

5.

The underside of the body was covered in scutes, like a crocodile or alligator.

63

Triceratops was a big animal but there has been discussion about how much it weighed. Adult specimens may have been as much as 26 ft. long and 10 ft. tall. Some scientists say they weighed about 6 tons, but others believe they could have been up to 13 tons in weight.

Like many dinosaurs, the *Triceratops* has had a bit of a makeover since it was first discovered. Luckily, fairly complete skeletons were found early on, but we now know it looked different than what earlier scientists thought. Earlier drawings made it look fat and tired. Its head was low and the tail dragged. The feet were flat on the ground. Now, scientists believe it held its head and tail higher and it was more muscular than fat.

1. After all this time, we still don't know exactly what the horns and frills were used for. Some *Triceratops* fossils have been found with healed bite marks (from *Tyrannosaurus rex*) on the crest, meaning that they may have used it for defense.

Another idea is that the crests were used to warm up or cool down the body in the same way elephants use their ears. Most scientists believe that even if they were sometimes used for defense or to help balance temperature, the most important use was probably for display.

Many animals use horns and crests for **courtship displays**, **territorial displays** and **species identification**.

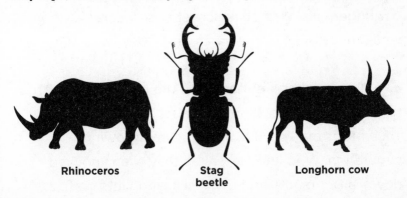

Rhinoceros   **Stag beetle**   **Longhorn cow**

Look at rhinos, stag beetles and cows which do similar things for display today.

Often, it was enough to have big horns or colorful crests, but sometimes *Triceratops* would fight with other *Triceratops*. Some fossils have been found with puncture marks in the skull and crest that perfectly fit the shape and size of a *Triceratops* horn, showing they did fight. Scientists believe that if they rammed each other head-on, their skulls and horns would have smashed. They think instead that *Triceratops* locked horns and wrestled.

2. When we see the fossil horns, we are not seeing the whole thing. In fossils, we just see what would have been bone. The horns of animals like cows, antelopes and ceratopsid dinosaurs have what we call a **bone core** beneath and a covering over the top. This would have been **made from keratin**, the same stuff that makes up our fingernails. With these coverings, *Triceratops* horns would have been even longer when they were alive.

3. The **head was quite low to the ground**, compared to some plant-munching dinosaurs like *Diplodocus*. *Triceratops* may have focused on low-growing vegetation. Who knows, maybe they even knocked down larger plants and trees, like elephants do today.

4. *Triceratops* had **strong limbs** that helped support its **massive body**. The forelimbs were shorter than the hind limbs and only had three claws. The hind limbs each had four claws.

5. Fossilized dinosaur skin is very, very rare. Skin imprints are more commonly found but are still rare. These happen when the skin presses against soft mud surrounding the body and the impression is fossilized.

A *Triceratops* fossil found in 2002 has some of the best-preserved skin seen in any dinosaur. There weren't just little pieces but huge chunks of skin, enabling scientists to see exactly what they would have looked like. On the underside, the body was **covered in scutes, like a crocodile** or alligator. The rest of the body was covered by small scales, like many other dinosaurs. But there were extra scales, mixed in with these small ones. These were about the size of an adult person's fist and were hexagon shaped. In the middle was a little hole.

6. These hexagonal scales may have held a secret *Triceratops* adaptation. We have absolutely no idea if this is really so as yet, but some scientists believe that each of these scales acted like an anchor for a long quill, like those of hedgehogs and porcupines. This idea comes from a *Triceratops* relative, the *Psittacosaurus*, from Asia. This horned dinosaur had quills around its tail and maybe *Triceratops* did too.

It's important to remember, though, that *Psittacosaurus* was a distant relative and *Triceratops* may not have looked like this at all. This is an ongoing debate in science and we may know very soon if *Triceratops* was covered in long spines.

True or false? We will find out . . .

CHAPTER 5

Dinosaur Domains

HABITATS AND ECOSYSTEMS

HABITATS AND ECOSYSTEMS

The *Triceratops* dinosaurs were herbivorous ceratopsids that first appeared in the fossil record around 68 million years ago, during the Late Cretaceous. By 66 million years ago, they were gone.

In places where *Triceratops* fossils are found, there are so many bits of horns, skulls, crests and teeth that scientists think they were probably the most common herbivorous dinosaurs from that time in that area. One researcher thinks that at the end of the Cretaceous, *Triceratops* represented over 80 percent of the large dinosaurs around.

Because so many *Triceratops* teeth have been found (and because they're pretty big), we're fairly sure they were eating tough, fibrous plants (and they were eating *lots* of them). There is disagreement over exactly what they ate – some think they ate things like palms while others think they mainly ate ferns.

You probably know that Earth looked very different in prehistoric times and that continents shifted and moved over millions of years, but did you know that there was just less land anyway? During most of the Cretaceous period, sea levels were higher than at any other time in

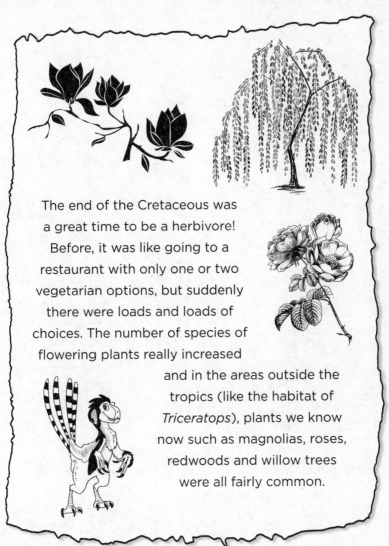

The end of the Cretaceous was a great time to be a herbivore! Before, it was like going to a restaurant with only one or two vegetarian options, but suddenly there were loads and loads of choices. The number of species of flowering plants really increased and in the areas outside the tropics (like the habitat of *Triceratops*), plants we know now such as magnolias, roses, redwoods and willow trees were all fairly common.

Earth's history. Nowadays, sea levels are 650–820 ft. lower than they were back in the Late Cretaceous. When *Triceratops* was alive, the Earth was warmer than

it is now. But across that time period, Earth did cool, meaning that the tropics were only around the area of the Equator (similar to today) and that northern and southern regions had different seasons across the year.

Many of the *Triceratops* fossils discovered have been found in what scientists call the Hell Creek Formation. Hell Creek stretches between Montana, North Dakota, South Dakota and Wyoming in North America.
It formed at the end of the Cretaceous when a system

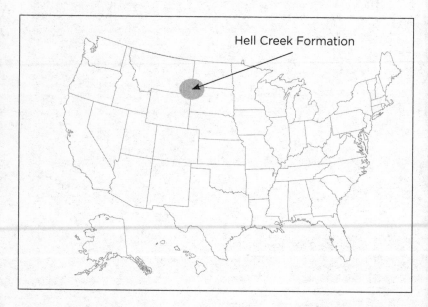

Hell Creek Formation

of rivers, estuaries and swamps left an area that is now rich in clay, mudstone and sandstone – all great for fossil preservation. The Hell Creek habitat would have been

During the Late Cretaceous period, the oceans were full of submerged mountain ranges. This made the water level much higher than it is today and meant that there were lots of shallow seas in North America, South America, Africa, Europe and Australia.

Because the sea level was so much higher then, there was less land. Today, land covers about 28 percent of Earth's surface, but in the Late Cretaceous, it covered just 18 percent.

one with freshwater and brackish rivers and lakes, with lots of ferns, palms and trees around the edges. The climate was subtropical but mild. During the year, there would have been no periods of cold, as we have in our winters.

The Hell Creek Formation is a world-famous site for fossils. As well as fossils from insects, plants, pterosaurs, plesiosaurs, mosasaurs, crocodiles, snakes, lizards, turtles, fish, amphibians and mammals, the area would have been full of dinosaurs, both in terms of numbers and different species.

Here are some of the dinosaur species found in the same area as *Triceratops* fossils:

Acheroraptor

Ornithomimus

Nanotyrannus

Pectinodon

Tyrannosaurus

Richardoestesia

Struthiomimus

Anzu

Ankylosaurus

Nedoceratops

Edmontonia

Edmontosaurus

Leptoceratops

Torosaurus

Parasaurolophus

Leptorhynchos

Pachycephalosaurus

So You Think You Know About Dinosaurs?

How many species of *Triceratops* were there?

•

How many toes did a *Triceratops* have
on its front feet?

•

How much did a *Triceratops* weigh?

•

In what period did *Triceratops* roam Earth?

•

Name three plants that were around
in *Triceratops*' time.

*All the answers are in the text
and at the back of the book.*

Inflatable Nose Balloons

Do a quick dino experiment and think of a *Triceratops* skeleton. What pops into your head?

Four legs and a stocky body?

Big horns? Big skull crest?

Anything else?

Did you think about their nostrils?

No?

Why not?

The nasal cavity (the nostrils and holes in the skull related to the nose) is big in the horned dinosaurs and especially the later ones such as *Triceratops*.

It only becomes obvious just how big the *Triceratops* nasal cavity is when you look at it alongside other dinosaur skulls. Have a look at these four skulls.

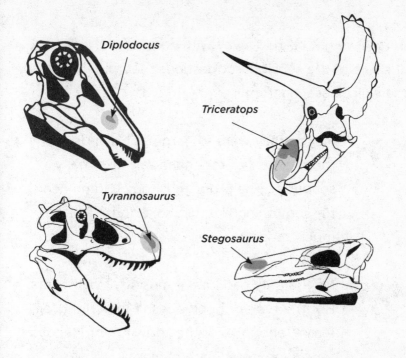

Diplodocus

Triceratops

Tyrannosaurus

Stegosaurus

They are from four different dinosaur species but have been made to look the same size, so that it's easier to compare the same parts of the different animals. The *Diplodocus*, *Stegosaurus* and *Tyrannosaurus* skulls all have nasal cavities roughly the same size. They aren't too big and there's nothing too surprising when you look at them. Now look at the *Triceratops* skull. The nasal cavity is huge. Much bigger than is needed for the actual nostrils. And in this area, there are lots of complicated bony structures that you don't see in other species. So, horned dinosaurs had huge nasal cavities, with some complex stuff going on around them.

Before we get carried away with crazy ideas, let's look at some of the sensible suggestions that might explain the weird nasal anatomy:

 Maybe they were for large salt glands, helping them get rid of too much salt (like many seabirds). The problem is they had no need for something like this, so it doesn't make much sense.

 Maybe they had lots of muscle attachments. But the type of bone doesn't look right (or strong enough) for the sort of thing needed for strong muscle attachments.

 Maybe the holes allowed space for lots of blood vessels, which in turn helped in temperature control. It's possible, because elephant ears, for example, do the same sort of thing, so it's not out of the question.

You might be thinking, "Well, who cares about the nose of a *Triceratops*?" but the huge nasal cavity might be behind the most amazing thing about this dinosaur. Maybe (just maybe) they had huge inflatable nose sacs that they used to either scare predators or display to others of their kind, such as males displaying to other males, or males trying to impress females.

We haven't been able to prove this yet, and not everyone agrees that these horned dinosaurs had huge inflatable nose balloons for display and communication, but it's possible. Have a look at the structures of the skull, consider the options and see what you think. This is an area of dinosaur science that is being discussed right now.

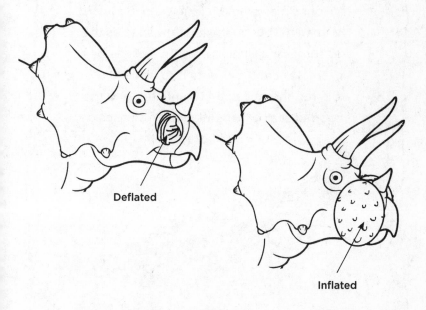

Deflated

Inflated

If it's correct, the *Triceratops* and other horned dinosaurs just got a lot, lot cooler.

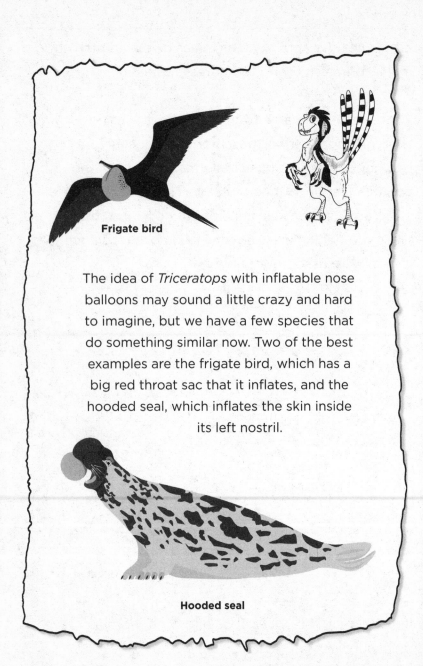

Frigate bird

The idea of *Triceratops* with inflatable nose balloons may sound a little crazy and hard to imagine, but we have a few species that do something similar now. Two of the best examples are the frigate bird, which has a big red throat sac that it inflates, and the hooded seal, which inflates the skin inside its left nostril.

Hooded seal

CHAPTER 6

Dodging Dinosaurs

EVOLUTIONARY ARMS RACE

EVOLUTIONARY ARMS RACE

An evolutionary arms race is a bit like a game with no real rules in which the loser can't start again, but gets injured or killed. The easiest way to think about it is like this – if a prey species evolves to make it easier to avoid a predator, then the predator evolves to make it easier to kill the prey. Then the prey evolves again and so does the predator . . .

But it's not always between species of predators and prey – sometimes the evolutionary arms race happens within a single species. An example is the red deer. These beautiful mammals have evolved a whole range of adaptations to make sure every male has the best chance of being dominant. They have big bony antlers, with lots of sharp and deadly pointed tips. They could fight with these but would risk serious injury or death. Sometimes it's easier to show off rather than fight and red deer do this. Usually the stag with the most spikes on its antlers will be dominant. But if not, red deer have a series of behaviors to test the strength of the other animal and to show off each animal's power. This should work, but if it doesn't, then maybe they will fight after all. Although we don't know for sure, social dinosaurs like *Triceratops* may have behaved in similar ways.

Sometimes, the biggest threat doesn't come from a predator but from another of its own kind. *Triceratops* faced this type of threat. Nothing could take down a fully grown adult male *Triceratops*, apart from another big male *Triceratops.*

THE BATTLE

There is a group of *Triceratops* by the river. The waters are flowing slowly by, with huge catfish and strange-looking sawfish swimming in the shallows between the long green weeds. The beach is wide and sandy and stretches along the river. Hundreds of *Triceratops* are gathered there in small groups, feeding on the different plants along the shoreline, with the young ones playing in the shallow waters. There are old and

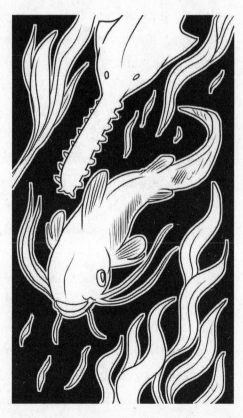

young animals, groups of females and mothers with babies. And there are males. Lots of them. There are many family groups, with up to 20 animals. Heading each group is an adult male. He defends his group and mates with the females, so that all the babies are his. With so much at stake, he will fight to the death.

A large group is defended by a "beach master," one of the largest males on the beach. He is a huge animal, weighing a little over 11 tons. His left horn is snapped off at the end, and he is missing a chunk of tail from where he was attacked by a *T. rex* when he was much younger. He has dominated this part of the beach for years. As he grazes on some soft ferns, he looks up and spots another male walking down the beach. The newcomer has no group of his own and is looking to challenge a male who already has a group. He wants a fight. The newcomer is younger than the beach master but still very big. Both males are highly aggressive.

The beach master walks along the shallows and stamps his foot, kicking up stones and splashing water. The newcomer stops for a second and kicks up sand too, deliberately walking with exaggerated stiff steps. They walk closer until they are within a few feet of each other, then the beach master bellows a challenge. The newcomer responds by roaring back, accepting the challenge.

Both know that
if they fight,
they risk injury
or death. So
instead, they
display, showing
off their strength
and power. They walk
side by side, shaking their heads as they lower them
close to the ground, before throwing them up high. Both
are looking at the other's horns and crest. Whoever has
the biggest horns and crest is probably the strongest –
it's what we call "honest signaling."

The beach master tosses his head from side to side,
kicking up sand with his hind feet, angrily slashing his tail
in the air. If the newcomer doesn't back down, a battle is
inevitable. Each male has a lot to fight for. They move in
and lock horns. They lean together, pushing into the sand,
their feet sinking. Each animal grunts and tries to force
the other to the ground to win the fight, but these two
are perfectly matched in strength.

As their horns are tightly locked, they swing around,

crashing about on the beach. Other *Triceratops* move out of the way. As they wrestle, the newcomer smashes into a baby, sending it flying into the water.

As the two big males crash together again, the beach master's horns scrape all the way along the face of the newcomer. Bleeding now, the newcomer breaks away and lunges at the beach master, trying to gouge his stomach to kill him.

The beach master swerves to avoid the deadly blow, and slips on a patch of slick wet weed on the stones in the shallows. He falls on one knee and is vulnerable. The newcomer rushes at him, ready to kill. He lifts his head to slam down with those horns.

Using all his strength, the beach master pushes himself up and raises his head, his horns straight, as the newcomer lunges. It happens in seconds and the newcomer realizes the danger he is in. He had been poised to kill the beach master, but now, the newcomer is instead throwing all his weight straight onto those horns.

The beach master twists his head and his long undamaged right horn pierces the newcomer through the chest. The horn hits a rib, snapping it in two, before it also breaks. The newcomer bellows in pain and rears back. The beach master's snapped horn remains inside, where it pierces a lung, causing massive injury.

The newcomer lies in the shallow water, breathing rapidly, while the beach master carries on displaying to any other males in the area who might want to challenge him. Blood flows from the dying newcomer, turning the shallow water red.

With huge aggressive males like these, physical fights are a last resort. They challenge and display to show their dominance, using rituals similar to those seen in red deer, but when the stakes are so high, fighting is sometimes inevitable. When two heavily armored, heavily weaponed males like these fight over territory or defend their groups, a fight can quickly turn deadly.

There is no proof that *Triceratops* behaved like this or displayed to each other, but many animals do today. Red deer stags walk side by side, roaring at each other; they show off their huge antlers and even pee on themselves to "smell tough." They attach clumps of plants and weeds to their antlers to make sure they look the biggest and scariest. See if you can find more ways animals display to each other.

Fossil
Finder

This might sound silly but when I was growing up, I had the idea that if I dug in my backyard, eventually I'd find a dinosaur. OK, stop laughing . . . I was little! But it leads to a serious question – why is it that you only find certain fossils in certain areas and sometimes, no fossils at all?

Well, first of all, some dinosaurs and other prehistoric species lived in very specific areas. It doesn't matter how long I look for a *Triceratops* fossil in the UK, I'm never going to find one . . . simply because they lived in what is now known as North America. The other reason is because some rock types contain fossils and some don't, and because you need to make sure the rock is the right age. That's right – all rock is old but there are different types of old.

THERE ARE THREE MAIN TYPES OF ROCK:

Sedimentary rock These rocks are made when mud, sand and pebbles are laid down, layer on top of layer. Over years and years, the pressure squashes these layers together and eventually turns them into rock. Limestone and

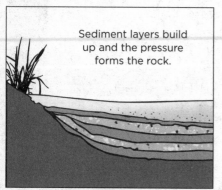

Sediment layers build up and the pressure forms the rock.

sandstone are good examples of sedimentary rocks. These rocks are great for fossils.

Igneous rock

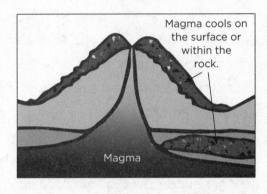

Magma cools on the surface or within the rock.

Magma

The word igneous comes from the Latin word meaning fire and this clue helps explain where igneous rock comes from. It starts off as magma, either from volcanoes or from within Earth. This cools and hardens to make igneous rock. Granite is an example of an igneous rock.

Metamorphic rock

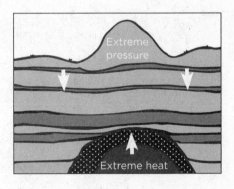

Extreme pressure

Extreme heat

This type of rock is formed when either sedimentary or igneous rock is changed because of extreme heat or extreme pressure. Slate, marble and schist are all examples of metamorphic rock. Sometimes there are fossils in these rocks but they are often squashed.

Usually, fossils are found preserved in sedimentary rocks. Because of the way the rock was made and because it doesn't really change that much over time, fossils are preserved well. Sandstone is made of tiny grains of eroded rock, and limestone is made up from tiny fossilized shells and skeletons from prehistoric plankton. Both these types of sedimentary rocks are great for finding fossils.

Now, all you need to do is to find which type of rock is where and how old that rock is. Where can you find Jurassic sedimentary rock that may contain giant marine reptiles like pliosaurs or rock from the Cretaceous period, full of ammonites and belemnites?

US

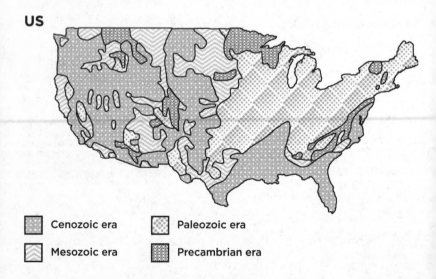

▦	Cenozoic era	▦	Paleozoic era
▨	Mesozoic era	▦	Precambrian era

Have a look at the map – the different patterns show the different types of rock where fossils can be found. Think about the fossils you would like to find and do a bit of detective work. If you really want to find an ammonite, it helps to know that they were only found in the Jurassic and Cretaceous periods. So there's no point in looking in rock from the Triassic period. Also, think about how that animal lived. Ammonites, for example, were marine animals, so look in places that were covered by the sea in prehistoric periods. This means it's a great idea to look at a site that used to be a Jurassic sea habitat and not a Jurassic freshwater river. Think about the age of the rock, the type of rock and how your fossil animal lived.

Here's a helpful list of some of the best fossils sites around the US and the type of rock you can find there.

Cenozoic era
Paleogene – Quaternary period
65 – 0 million years ago

Big Sandy Formation, Arizona
Blanco Formation, Texas
Bone Valley Formation, Florida

Mesozoic era
Cretaceous period 145 – 65 MYA

Austin Chalk, Texas
Cedar Mountain Formation, Colorado
Dinosaur Valley State Park, Texas
Hell Creek Formation, Montana, North Dakota, South
Dakota, Wyoming

Mesozoic era
Jurassic period 200 – 145 MYA

Aztec Sandstone, California
Bone Cabin Quarry, Wyoming
Dinosaur State Park, Connecticut

Paleozoic era
Carboniferous period 359 – 299 MYA

Bakken Formation, Montana
Linton Formation, Ohio

Paleozoic era
Silurian and Devonian periods 444 – 359 MYA

Bainbridge Formation, Missouri
Quarry Mountain Formation, Oklahoma
Rose Hill Formation, New York

Quiz Answers

Page 40

How many species of birds are there around today?

About 10,000.

Was a *Triceratops* larger or smaller than an elephant?

Smaller.

How many species of horned dinosaurs do we currently know about?

65.

How many horns did a *Triceratops* have and where?

Three – one above the nose and two above the eyes.

Where have most *Triceratops* fossils been found?

Hell Creek Formation.

Page 78

How many species of *Triceratops* were there?

Two – *Triceratops horridus* and *Triceratops prorsus.*

How many toes did a *Triceratops* have on its front feet?

Five.

How much did *Triceratops* weigh?

13 tons.

In what period did *Triceratops* roam Earth?

Late Cretaceous.

Name three plants that were around in *Triceratops'* time?

Magnolia, rose, redwood, willow.

How many did you get?

Glossary

Jog your memory here.

Adaptation A feature in a living organism that increases its chances of either surviving or breeding (or both). An adaptation can be physical (like the camouflaged stripes of a zebra) or a type of behavior (like lions hunting in groups).

Brackish Water that is a mix of fresh water with a little bit of salt water. Brackish water is often found in estuaries and tidal rivers.

Ceratopsid Any one of the horned dinosaurs. *Triceratops*, *Titanoceratops*, *Torosaurus* and *Styracosaurus* are all examples of ceratopsid dinosaurs. All ceratopsids had a frill and at least one horn on the skull.

Dominant Where one individual animal has power over another animal.

Ecologist A scientist who studies ecology.

Ecology An area of science where the focus is on the relationships between different species (of animals or plants) and their relationship with their environment.

Erode Where land, soil or rock is worn away over time because of the effects of wind, rain or ice.

Herbivore An animal that has a diet made up only of plants.

Maastrichtian This was the five-million-year period of time at the very end of the Cretaceous period. It started 72.1 million years ago and finished 66 million years ago. Well-known dinosaurs such as *Tyrannosaurus rex*, *Triceratops* and *Velociraptor* were all from this time.

Nasal Anything to do with the nose and the area around it.

Quadrupedal This describes any animal that walks on four legs. Cats, dogs, cows and dinosaurs such as *Triceratops* are all examples of quadrupedal animals.

Taxonomy The area of science that focuses on putting things in groups according to how closely related they are to each other. It is a way of classifying different species and different groups of organisms.

PICTURE CREDITS

NOTE from **SCOTT HARTMAN**:

Triceratops: The *Triceratops* skeletal is based on a specimen that is mounted at the Wyoming Dinosaur Center in Thermopolis, WY. WDC LF-001 is much less famous than some other skeletals, but I had excellent access to it while I was illustrating.

Visit

www.bengarrod.co.uk

for lots more about
dinosaurs.

MEET DR. BEN GARROD

Dr. Ben Garrod is an evolutionary biologist, which means he studies how different animals change over time. He has worked worldwide with chimpanzees, whales, sharks and dinosaurs.

As a child growing up by the sea he fell in love with nature. He found his first fossil when he was very small and has loved dinosaurs ever since.

Ben is a TV presenter and a Teaching Fellow at Anglia Ruskin University in the UK.

bengarrod.co.uk

So You Think You Know About...
DINOSAURS?

HAVE YOU GOT THEM ALL?